After The Rain

Also by I.B. Iskov

ENIGMA OF THE MIND: SECOND EDITION

ANXIETY ATTACK

BLACK AND WHITE

To Raia,
With Best wishes,

I.B. Iskov

After The Rain

Poems

EDMONTON, ALBERTA, CANADA
SNOWAPPLE PRESS

To Order Direct:
  Snowapple Press
  Box 66024, Heritage Postal Outlet
  Edmonton, Alberta, T6J 6T4

National Library of Canada Cataloguing in Publication Data

Iskov, I. B., (date)
  After the rain

ISBN 1-895592-26-7

I. Title.
PS8567.S59A72 2001   C811'.54   C2001-910811-7
PR9199.3.I82A72 2001

"Snow Apple" -- a North American variety of apple having red-streaked fruit.

☻
     ACID FREE PAPER - Recycled paper produced with the alkaline
process of papermaking, resulting in a **non-acid**, environmentally friendly product
that has long lasting, non-fading archival properties. The paper used in this
publication should meet the requirements for permanence of paper for printed
library materials.

First Printing, 2001
    1   2   02 01

MANUFACTURED AND PRINTED IN CANADA

FOR RACHEL

FOREWORD

In reading I.B. Iskov's poetry, one is struck by the enthusiasm and energy of spirit that infuse her work. More importantly, the reader is impressed with how seamlessly the poet and person who wrote the poetry are interwoven. To experience Iskov's poetry is to know the person. One would have to say that the poet and the person are the same. This is rare among poets. So often what poets write may be quite apart from who they are, either because they affect a persona or their work is steeped in craft and poetic devices. One can criticize Iskov for not being too advanced in her craft or not having a facility with the subtleties and nuances of our English language. However, many poets do not possess that natural gift whereby poet and poetry are one.

We don't have to compare Iskov to an Al Purdy or Leonard Cohen, two poets of great skill who dedicated their lives to their craft. Purdy and Cohen were what they wrote. Masters of the craft, they achieve a simplicity through the most important force in their arsenal, being the natural force of who they are, because ultimately honesty and truth are what separate the poets from the pretenders.

I.B. Iskov could not be a pretender if she tried. Honesty and truth shine from her work. Therefore, she draws on the deep compassion, love, and pain she has lived and endured, not to depress the reader or in an attempt to enlighten us, but to share who she is and her personal truth. And what Iskov is, we who know her as a person and a poet, are impressed by.

Iskov has a solid grounding in rhyme and forms of metrical poetry. This is also rare among contemporary poets who write chopped-up prose, and stick it into lines and stanzas that lack any concept of scansion or rhythm. She has a voice which is totally her own. I always enjoy and am occasionally surprised by Iskov's poetry. I have the feeling she can accomplish anything she desires in writing poetry. She can play at it or get serious. Either way, we are treated to someone whose love for poetry inspires. Read I.B. Iskov and know a fine, unique poet who is also that way as a person.

Ted Plantos, October, 2000.

Contents

A Distant Rain

After The Rain

Acknowledgements

Many of the poems in this book have appeared in the following magazines and anthologies:

IN CANADA

Break-through! Quarterly Magazine; Tupperware Sandpiper; An Invisible Accordion, Postal Code, Strong Winds, Canadian Poetry Association Anthology; *People's Poetry Newsletter; Undertow; Daytripping In Southwestern Ontario; In A Nutshell; The Lexicon,* York University; *Diviners; Our Voice/Notre Voix; We Are T.O.P.S.* Newsletter; *Teak Roundup Prose & Poetry Quarterly; Henry's Creature: Poems and Stories on The Automobile,* Black Moss Press; *Destinations & Discoveries In Midwestern Ontario; Museletter & Writes Of Spring Anthology,* League of Canadian Poets; *Earle Birney-A Tribute, Prism International.*

IN THE U.S.A.

Poet's Fantasy, Rice Lake, Wisconsin
Street News, New York, N.Y. www.heartandfire.com

The following poems appeared in the *Outreach Connection Newspaper*, Toronto, Ontario:

A Rainbow's In the Gutter, election day or Uncle Bobby, i only have a brother, in the mall, Mary-Beth, Job Hunting, my mother to me, my universe, On Mental Illness, secret customs, Sheltered Death, The August Leaves, the boys, The Budgie, The Dream, the homeless market, The Homeless, the market, The Sea of Silence, turning grey in summer, upwards on windy stairs, where would you want to be?

On Mental Illness was featured in a video for the *1988 CBC Telefest.*

A Distant Rain

weather gems

from mounds of fresh snow
the water breaks
through icy clouds
like a small voice

tiny little crystal beads
cluster like
transparent ruby raspberries

there is ambiguity
in the water bubbles
glistening like fresh fruit
ripened by the sun

both have taken hours
to perfect their ideal state
in colour and in praise

for the colour white

part 1

the ceiling
a cloudless sky
indistinct eyes stare
completely
no cure
for the emptiness

doctors in white
nurses in white
patients in white
their antiseptic dreams a vapour
locked up in white
manila folders

part 2

the church wedding
dressed in white
mints that taste green
chocolate that tastes brown
devoured by hungry eyes
white laughing
toothpaste teeth that taste like red

part 3

i leave white alone
but it follows me everywhere
leaving no trace
of colour behind

**small poems which act as a guide
on how to be an authority figure**

For L.S. -- you know who you are

1. Who

an authority figure comes
in various shapes, sizes and colours
they can be male and/or female
there is no religious barrier
all members of the human race
over the age of five
are eligible
however
there are certain rules and guidelines
you must follow

2. How

to be an authority
is obvious
you must know everything
or just pretend to
throw your weight around
that doesn't mean to insinuate you need to
be the least little bit
overweight
it only means
you have to be highly
opinionated about every subject
practice snobbery
on a full time basis

3. When

you have established
yourself as an authority
figure you can act
like an ethereal being
elevate others
to stardom
or banish them
into failure
in other words
you can play god
if you want others
to believe you are
omnipotent
let your words be published
somewhere   you can
truthfully claim
to be immortal

4. Dress Code

although it is optional
an authority figure can
wear a chaplinesque moustache
and/or a grey flannel uniform
it is vogue to own
a hundred pairs of shoes
use them to step on everyone
in the name of politics
don't bother to wear a crown
no one will bow down to you
but they will kiss ass
to gain favour   once

they have what they need
you can be assured
there is always room
for one more
authority figure.

5. Where

authority figures can be found
in most businesses
in the complaint department
just try to complain
to an authority figure
you can't win
they got their education
at city hall

6. Proper Etiquette

squint your eyes and smile
when you talk to people
when you lie to them
they'll never know
the difference
judge everyone
on a first impression
never give anyone a second
chance
when you are finished
tearing down and destroying
anyone who rubs you
the wrong way
don't be surprised
when you hear a voice
whisper *drop dead*
into your ear

7. While On Vacation

no stone statue
or plastic doll can act
as an authority figure
they have no voice
although they have other attributes
to be good contenders
as an authority figure
for instance
they also have no heart
and no conscience

8. Place of Business

make sure your office is on the top
floor   no other floor will do
even if people don't look up to you
they will have to look up to your office
from the ground
floor   having an office up high
will make you feel like
a top notch authority figure
or just pretend

9. Who

an authority figure should have followers
after all what good is power
without adoration   since a pedestal
is too cumbersome to take with you
everywhere   you definitely need
a few admirers to put you on one
just call yourself an intellectual
and other intellectuals will laud you
and applaud you

10. Image Builder

an authority figure should commit
one act of kindness
you don't have to escort anyone
across the street
we have boy scouts for that
congratulating a rival
when they steal your coveted prize
would be nice
or helping someone realize
their fondest dream
even if you can't stand
their silly walk
or the way they hold their tongue
don't worry
if you find it impossible
to carry out one small good deed
this is very hard for
a bigot
a stigmatizer and
a pedagogical wizard
no one will think
post modern
they'll just pretend

slipping back

i own an old worn out pair of slippers
from my youth
when pretty firm and soft
pink pastel
matched the Mary Quant and mohair
i wore
on dates

blue velvet memories
stored in the comfort
of my closet

the homeless market

there is no deficit
according to the
T.H.E.
(Toronto Homeless Exchange)
managed by
high unemployment
and low government spending
the homeless market
is stabilized
and rises steadily
(this stock is hot as a pistol)

if you haven't seen the signs,
take yourself to Bay Street
where the fastest growing commodities
beg for your investments

my words

once my words were salt water
and i was an ocean
once my words were gun shots
and i was an assassin
once my words were smooth pebbles
and i was a lonely road
when my words became a gentle breeze
the air turned menopausal

space

there is a space
you have to know
there is a space
you have never touched
in between every breath
there is a space
consumed by words
quickly buried
in a cryptic coffin
among the dead
of an untold space

head shaved
wires hooked
feeding
the catatonic
body cries out for one
small blank space

there is none

i only have a brother

for gary

when i was ten i traveled on a train
with many Catholic nuns
i ran up and down the aisles
cheerfully singing
"hi sister, hi sister, hi sister"

i always wanted a sister

What I Said When He Asked Me Why I like Poetry

hypnosis
is a desert

exhaustion
is a place

oh pilgrim
I'm caraway

oh foetus
I'm reckless

the waiting room

a panorama of scars
etched in stucco
frames the finger
printed ceramic
scrubbed daily

slender arms of steel
shoulder one another
like an army of dancers
their synchronized legs
cautiously positioned
on hard wood injured
like the wounds seeking attention
by the im-
patient no longer waiting
in the room

scherzo

the epanalepsis of affection
occurs sporadically
in parked cars

every time two people fall
for each other, three little words
are constantly whispered

"got a condom?"

the token saint

discarded
in last year's sentiment
shreds of dancing words
mangle
a naked pendulous web
envelope
the crumpled cupid
final plastic whispers
fill the pallid air

no blood stains
the passionate dust
only a distant rain

sings a crystal
soliloquy mourns
the translucent
lacerated heart

After The Rain

A Rainbow's In The Gutter

A rainbow's in the gutter.
It fell from lack of hope.
It lies there, broken-hearted.
It has no strength to cope.

Its colours fading quickly.
They're slipping down the drain.
Neglected and forgotten,
The rainbow leaves no stain.

Its death won't change the world.
No one cares what's in the gutter.
We choose to ignore the needy,
When all they need is bread and butter.

If it rains hard in your world
And you need help from anyone,
You could end up like the rainbow
In a gutter, all alone.

aftermath

twisted limbs mangled in the sickly
debris trapped trees
desperate convicts
careening in a scabrous prison

warped telephone poles claw
the callous sky

country homes spit insulation
on flooded lawns
shallow graves for soiled clothing
at every intersection

police cars vacantly guard
the looted shops

canvas shelters and portable toilets
blossom like over-grown weeds
on confused soil

anxious helicopters pulsate over food lines
bottled water rationed
in controlled chaos

could it be

could it be
the semibreve
of reverberation
from the car engine
is a novel classic

could it be
the notifiable
jam session
is the severance
of work and pay

it could be
that I drive
myself
too hard

every so often
the long winded trail
I explore
on purpose
has no climax
to scout

I reshuffle
my feet
and play the engine
like an old song
reverberating over
and over
and over
again

the embrocation

i could really really use
a good old fashioned
freshly home made
smooth as chocolate
cool as the morning mist
delightful as ragwort
satisfying as a cherry
lollipop embrocation

i would be a willing subject
expose my sin
-ews and my private
innermost sensitive
body parts
to a real macho
devotee of health
-y capillaries

his fine tuned fingers
would muscle music
in lilting rotations
up and down my spine

Larry

i sit on the green velvet
and watch you
and the T.V.
night after night
the new carpet lies
on the floor quietly
begging to be noticed

the T.V. screen is alive
with colour
on a wave of noise
crowds and commentaries
an endless ritual
of struggle and competition

you are stretched out
on the big couch
the emerald pillows suffocate
under your head
they too are quiet
and content to wait
for your perfect snore
and cradle your glasses
no matter how boring it is
during the commercials

i coyly snuggle
in the warmth of your neck
and press soft wet kisses
on your tired lips

genrecide

my bookcase leans
close offering
rows and rows
dust covered
literature
hiding in old jackets

like homeless men
squatting
in crowded spaces
vacant words
starve in volumes
suffering faltering spines
senile metaphors
forget time
like a cancelled sitcom

countless pages wither
from lack of exercise
and suffer from
literaeporosis
with yellow wrinkled
passages
entered long ago

i could bury my books
in cardboard coffins
and use the shelves
for my CD's and VHS movies
but that would be genrecide

On Mental Illness

Shadows on the ceiling.
Faces in the night.
Monsters in my closet.
Huge dogs that growl and bite.

Voices calling out to me.
They live inside my head.
I wish that they would go away
And bother someone else instead.

Is someone right behind me?
I feel them breathing down my neck?
Is someone 'round the corner?
Would you please go and check?

I wish I wasn't like this.
I wish I was like you.
Then nothing could stand in my way
Of being normal, too.

Sheltered Death

In memory of Eugene Upper, who froze to death in a bus shelter

one thin blanket
shields the cold
snap
in a glass house
no curtains   no door
shield the moon
with the eyes of death

sheltered death is like an oven
brings nurturing heat
to the frost
bitten slowly
melts away life
until all that is left
is one thin blanket
shielding the cold
snap

The Dream

i vividly recall
a sunny day
curled up
in the gutter
wearing checkered trousers
i wouldn't
be caught dead in

you came over
(it had to be you
though i couldn't see
your face)
i'd know
those pants anywhere

you took out some coins
from your pocket
threw them on me

it was too late for change

The Homeless

Living inside an uncertain world
Their dreams in a paper bag.
Sleeping in places you wouldn't dare.
It's the burden of life that they drag.

Parched veins dry into a complex of cobwebs
And assimilate to their graves.
Nothing to hold onto -- Nothing.
They drown in Society's waves.

The lights of the city shine brightly
Over the streets of despair.
Living outside, hungry and sick,
Winds of apathy blow through the air.

Souls huddled in darkened doorways.
The only shelter they find.
Bodies inflicted with moss-covered pain.
Rejection is locked in their minds.

In the cold grey dawn of tomorrow,
The homeless silently die
in a world that offers no faith.
Can anyone please explain why?

secret customs

they cruise down muddy roads
strong men with hard shiny rocks
adorn each knuckle like candied popcorn
each one a social paradox

they crash through sound proof walls
to kill the pain   to please the ladies
gripping their sweat in both hands
lined up cursing demons from Hades

they can be found dancing on Yonge Street
front of A & A's   a reggae tune
sold to unscrupulous dealers
smuggled in from Vera Cruz last june

there is a black market there
they have their own special rates
one is for the needle
one is for the united states

The Soul and Spirit of The Street

for Indio, Editor of Street News in New York

you've seen them
with tired eyes and hands
clutching useless treasures
with hunger for a friend

you've heard them
ramble empty thoughts
with empty stomachs
empty pockets
empty lives

you've given them
a dream to share
a smile to bank on
a corner to turn
their lives around

The Sea of Silence

Lost in an ocean filled with fear.
My thoughts immersed, like sunken ships.
Broken dreams and shattered hopes
Are locked within my frozen lips.

The sea of silence captures me.
An endless rhythm in my brain.
Chained to the waves of misery.
Groping for my life in vain.

A puppet in the hands of fate.
Glued to the strings of destiny.
Dancing to a demon's tune.
A cruel and heartless melody.

Like the wind, a silent breeze
Carrying all my memories.
Scattering leaves of shame and scorn
in swirling, falling pillories.

My screams engulfed in salty tears.
They fill the ocean of my soul.
A prisoner in the sunken ships.
No flag of hope upon the pole.

where would you want to be?

in an office building
on Finch Avenue
a derelict sleeps
in the men's room
in front of the urinals
like a beached whale

when no one is watching
he turns on the faucets
lets the cool reach his dry mouth
and empty stomach
until he becomes like the water
flowing in and out
of the lavatory
and the building

staggering
isn't it?

gonna wipe away my tears
for Jack & Jean

cfgm 1310 country raydee oh
aired ditties of grief and glory
from gene autrey to glen campbell
one after another
like gunshots
spent on the streets of Laredo

i envisioned rhinestone
boots blue suede
texas hat and matching vest

the treasured geetar
strummed by the campfire
under a star-spangled sky

i strung along
like an old cowhand
eager to be the sidekick
in a john wayne western

oh wha oh wha oh wha
did you make this cowpoke cry
roped my tenderfoot heart
with a twangy lasso

i was hog-tied to country music

Cannibal Run On Steeles

I board the bus
on Steeles Avenue
blood-shot eyes
ooze the bleak
the rain drizzles
saliva
through the windows

the bus driver
never looks back
he knows
his motorized cauldron
is heated up
in conversation

the passengers crammed
together complain
the ride is not poetry

in motion
the large metal belly
abundant with human flesh
consumed with newspapers, novels,
billboard signs
ingesting and digesting
other faces

lips move like buses
slow and steady
stopping for fresh words
like passengers
the phrases come and go
and I never remember
the funny joke
the comment made in passing
just another voice in the crowd

I spoon faces
with my tongue
distinguish sentences
for breakfast
forgetting what I swallowed
by supper time

i told you the sky is agnostic

i sing a chronic ritual
bewitched by the morning moon
secure in the secret reflection

inside the day's hungry hours
my mouth opens constellations
an uncertain atmosphere

i solemnly avoid touch
impossible to embrace enchantment
a fool's opaque breath

ankle deep
i pry the surface of the air
before the light dies

my eyes suck moments
of pleasure beneath a silent sun
surrounded by windblown ashes

i told you the sky is agnostic
piously anchored
above ambiguous islands

old woman jogging

in the autumn
as your days grow shorter
you are up at dawn
like a little bird
dressed in the blue
breeze
on swift feet
to the tune on my radio

i struggle
through the oncoming slow
down   unable to rush
in the rush hour
your straight slim agile
perfectly tuned body
in better shape
than mine

the boys

for Dimitri, kicked to death in a swarming

not soldiers
not hit men
not *Nazis*
you would expect
to kill in a moment
of anger

when boys get rough
with other boys
in the playground
(mother always told me
to play in the park
where it was safe)
it was all in fun
it was a competition thing
not a game to die for

soft brown eyes
a dancing smile
robbed of life at fifteen
by the boys
wanting his last dollar
stealing his last breath

the boys
craving the drugs
hiding their sin
in playgrounds
lying
in wait for their next victim

Mary-Beth

Becky had a dolly
She'd hold and rock and sing.
She always kept it with her.
It was her favourite thing.

They'd play house together
And include the family dog.
It was a pure-bred Doberman
Whose name was Polly Wog.

One day Polly Wog took the dolly
Out in the yard to play.
Becky was at school.
She went for half a day.

The dog chewed up the dolly
And then ripped off her head.
Becky cried and cried
When she found her dolly dead.

Polly Wog was taken to the pound
And put to death,
For Becky's favourite dolly
Was her sister Mary-Beth.

the computer class

still half asleep
slipping
into sweatshirt and jeans
this middle-aged school girl
rushes head first
to the computer class

after adjusting my girdle
and resting
coffee on the desk,
i finally wake up
the computer

my greying head
to one side,
i cautiously clutch
the micro
soft mouse

like the remote i
initiate the T.V. screen

54

menu is offered
with no appetizers,
main courses or desserts
my palate is tempted
with an excel
lent spread
sheet

my IBM Selectric two brain
isn't ready for
F2 Wisdom
and the tools i need to master
the computer class
can't be found in the toolbar

give me back my magical kingdom

i entered the magical kingdom
full of promise
wondered how long
i could stay

i sat in the *Chair*
hardly empty
from the last grateful princess
quickly evicted
for not paying enough
attention to detail

i struggled to hold on
to the dream of fortune
but the flames of karma
singed my face
humble ashes of reason
settled at my feet

i am in a different kingdom now
not magical but finite
with stars that offer
a lesser wish come true

live with no crown
no halo and
no monster   crawling
to my bed
my nights hold the elixir
of the magical kingdom
captive in memory
to escape the boredom
of my reality

give me back my magical kingdom
let me once again
feel the embrace of gold
velvet on silver wheels
and coast along happily
ever after
if only for a little while

The Tumult and The Shouting

out of the queue
like a thunderbolt
indestructible and forever young
the Adonis quarterback
vigorously tears up the stadium
the coveted treasure
locked under his arm
swiftly ejects the inflated leather
half way across the country

burning with an unquenchable
desire to win
the battle of the game
ivy league soldiers in padded uniforms
huddle before the scrimmage
numbers are fired ammunition

iron fists and hearts of steel
the circle of comrades
ready to die
on the playing field

with a snap and a shaddle
football rhythm is played
with vigorous sophistication
the bulky athletes on their toes
like Rudolf Nureyev smooth
effortless   always in balance

sculptors   models   hard   muscular
perfect bodies undulating like snakes
at a garden party
the fans lounge
in the bleachers tackle hot-dogs
first down beer

awards night

the popsicle man
constantly hugs the microphone
his sandpaper voice
scratches my body
static words dandruff
my feet
all night long
his smooth round bowling ball
eyes roll over me

hundreds of people
line up for a prize
Popsicle Pete's jokes
are muffled by the scratching
coins dance
on lottery tickets

silver and gold
trophies disappear
one by one sighs of disappointment
slide across the floor
slam against the wall

heaven's teller

i have often wondered where my soul will end up after i die i
imagine what i will find at the end
of the rainbow   who will be there
waiting for me?   is there an ultimate judge
to decree and proclaim my fate?
what secret information is being stored
about my life in that big filing cabinet in the sky?
is the ethereal being eager to pass the verdict
a bank teller?   imagine dying with your bank balance
at an all time low
you close your eyes for the last time   only
to be doomed to an infinity of drudgery
in a hot oven
it's what i go through now every day in my kitchen

i suppose as long as i have no cheques
to cash in when i am cashing in
should make everything all right   right?
and even if i did need to cash a cheque at the Pearly Wicket
what other bank could i possibly go to?
Satan's Trust?
i wonder what kind of credit rating he would give
i must remember to leave my personal cheques at home
the only thing i plan to take with me when i die is
my name

Job Hunting

inside my shoes
the air suffocates
the laces disengage
tongues collapse
executives are speechless

the want ads crowd my head
like rush hour traffic
a bumper crop of cars continuously
drive through
countless doors opening
no vistas of opportunities

in the evening I remove my shoes
heavy with responsibilities
and miserable
from lack of sleep

my adversaries'
over-bearing feet
perform in shoes
as large as sleep
aggressive
like rush hour traffic
continuously
job hunting

monday morning

comes much too early
the almost dark sky yawns
before the waking sun
hungry for light

the air is loud with cold
the morning current
makes me shudder like a leaf

on a windy day
i cling to corners
where the heat vents
frustration
belting out
the same old song
kindled by the furnace

every November i am sick
of would-be frost and snow
bundle up in winter clothes
trek across the frigid
miles in my half-frozen
car grateful for the hot
cup of coffee
fuel for my shivering body

my universe
for Vivian

green and white
velvet sculptures
fade discretely
in the morning sun

the silver dust
sprinkles soft
on mahogany
while swollen fingers
embrace the slender needle
and play a silent song of silk

the embroidery sings
in tranquil tones
of earth and sky

i sit barefoot
in the picture
dig my splendid toes
in the gentle browns
like a gardener
in a tropical oasis

i patiently create
my universe
the eternal stitches
a small immortal gesture
not to be forgotten
like a tender lullaby
and a kiss

the ethical expatiation of the fairy tale

once upon a time
far, far away
the big bad wolf howled
hungrily in the meadow

beside a babbling brook
in a quaint candy cottage
the wicked witch cackled
stirring her black cauldron
while tiny bearded men
in green cowled cloaks
kept the fire burning

exactly at midnight
the hungry wolf
the wicked witch
and the tiny bearded men
sat around the fire and chanted

*"maybe we're hooded and hairy,
maybe we're homely and scary,
but we're working each day,
earning our pay,
happily ever after"*

The August Leaves

The August leaves gently fall
On the grass beneath the trees.
They sway and glide in rhythm
To the music of the breeze.

Their dance of Spring and Summer
In sunshine and in rain
Is swiftly done in unison
And always lost in vain.

The Autumn chill grows colder still
And winter steals away
A time of pleasant weather
When children love to play.

The August leaves wave farewell
To the flowers soon to die.
Like soldiers on the battlefield,
They too, refuse to cry.

They weave a golden blanket
To conceal the ground below.
Their efforts to protect the grass
Are smothered in deep snow.

Their hues of red and orange
Paint the sunsets in the sky.
They soar across the meadows
Like the monarch butterfly.
When Winter's term is over
In April's springtime glow,
The leaves return to decorate
Every place they grow.

total nightmare

the sound of death
screams through the open
blinds

am I dreaming wide
awake while the moon
pretends to sleep?

I ignore fatigue
not wanting slumber
to confirm
how tired I really am
I confine my
self to a jigsaw puzzle
trying to piece
what's left of the night

the morning will take forever

the sun will shine
on the sadness of the day
while I chew fingernails
in the same room
I paced in
the night before

The Crystal Rose
For Carol

not just another rose
that blooms
year after year
soft white velvet
and golden honey
sweetness

paper thin
petals like a butterfly's
carefully crafted
glass wings
in the rain

i can never embrace
the unyielding struggle for survival
i can only secretly admire
the quiet strength of the crystal rose
gallantly fighting for a space
among the garnets and the sapphires

but every rose must face the wind and rain
while everything else falls apart

Holocaust Cemetery
On visiting the Zaglembier Monument

grass and mud mingle
in trodden sorrow
around the granite

beloved names
of the dead
etched in Yiddish
like a story by Sholem Aleichem
written in Auschwitz

the engraved columns
bitterly sleep
on a slate grey landscape
in the orphaned park
without a voice
or a dream

the sun is buried too
under swollen clouds
the compressing sky
nears tears
and the wind clings
to my legs
like a frightened child

the air is in pain
its dull white grasping breath
makes the minutes crawl
in naked trembling silence

i never watch T.V.

i prefer to daydream
behind auburn bricks
resting tired elbows
on the cherrywood
in my Wedgwood blue

yesterday's conversations
circle my brain
like the patterns on china
familiar antiques antiquating
in a home sweet home

the crystal goblets
reflect my prismatic memories
the crayoned walls
the spilled milk
time-worn stains
on my porcelain
reveries
in still life

The Florida Condo

for my other mother, Frances

nestled among the man-made
lakes, palm trees and
the elderly only
a cat-walk away
a high exchange rate
of snowbirds and snowflakes
relax
in the Florida condo

bright tropical flowers bloom
on couches
in the filtered Florida sunshine
seasoned golfers trudge slowly
over the lush green
accompanied by hungry ducks
begging for a hand-out

and no matter which two weeks
I choose to bask in the dangerous rays
by the heated pool
at the Florida condo,
the sky is grey and cloudy
and it rains day and night
until I return to frosty Canada

Lost and Found

a familiar breeze
around the corner
the trees lounge
in the misty afternoon
for weeks
a young man sits
on a hard and dirty sidewalk
searching for a hand-out

each minute is final
the day presents the blue
absence of clouds
meandering and unimportant
like the young man begging

i have come and gone before
down the tired sidewalk
when the night was alive
with stars and my youth

the truth is here
and will stay humble
unless the breeze dies
and the promise of night
is found once more

Ziggy the Piggy

Ziggy the piggy lives in a sty.
He wallows in slop
He just loves to flop.
He's in love with a mop
I call Sweetie Pie.

He grunts and he snorts
Whenever he's in the mood.
I don't mean for food.
And would you think I'm rude
If I told you in sex he cavorts?

The chickens all hide in their coops
When Ziggy cums around.
Sweetie Pie is found
Thrust noisily to the ground
While Ziggy's tail does loop-de-loops.

The roosters all wink at each other.
They fluff their feathers twice their size
Familiar with the sounds of paradise
Which cascade in the starry skies
And shame each worried mother.

When Ziggy has reached his climax
He saunters back to his pen.
He joins the other men
Who can't understand his yen
For a mop which smells like Borax.

in the mall

plastic trees sway
under the halogen
sky glows
down busy aisles

the neon grins
wide yellow and white
above the paper
eyes in store front
windows boasting
sale after sale after sale

squeezing through
crowds like an orange
on the juicer dripping
sweat in weak
air conditioned spaces
leased by the square foot

the eager entrepreneurs
cool as mint toothpaste
for only ninety-nine cents

and i thought i was a mall rat

the hungry conception

words crept through
the bedroom window
on noisy spider legs
danced under the ceiling
their webs capturing light
between silver and moon
revealing intricate secrets

they hung over me
in heavy shadows
like woollen blankets
smothering my dreams
converging into one
huge appetite
for stars and chocolate

my mother to me

my mother to me
is not a scholar
she laboured long
and hard delivering
in seams and back
seams sweating
in stifling factories
for decades
her union
never went on strike

my mother complained
she never owned a doll
i am her perfect goddess
even after braces
eye operations
and breast surgery

my mother to me
is a block of wood
sturdy and porous
and i am her
exquisite carving

Ontario in the Spring

If you take a trip through Ontario
In April, May or June,
The morning dew and sunshine
Will sing their country tune.

The farmland stretches to the Sun
With quilted patchwork soil.
Cows and horses quietly graze
As farmers daily toil.

Century homes are nestled
In little towns along the way.
The balconies and gumwood trim
Are a part of the display.

Bed and Breakfasts and quaint Motels
Wait patiently to greet you.
Friendly folks with hometown jokes
Are always glad to meet you.

The highway's a silver ribbon
Securely wrapped around the terrain.
It leads you on a memorable tour
And then back home again.

poetry grounds

i've made a path
it rhymes
(the past is always present)
my own cough rhymes
i can't stop
it's chromatic

the path is long
and leads to different paths
like the human body
with arms and fingers
stretching, grasping
pens, needles, manna

the path i walk on
is surrounded
by expectations
in full bloom

this is my garden,
my ornamental grounds
for poetry

The Loneliness of The Poet

few people ask me to recite at dinner
though heaven knows I have poems
fresh and ready made, like salad
eager to serve and toss up
bleak and haunting imagery
but I have to eat with my mouth closed

i often cleanse my body and my thoughts
at the same time I can use the soap
and quietly ramble off a poem
the bathtub is a vessel for my words
naked and soaking wet
the poem dissipates with the steam

i try to find a listener
but all the 1-800 numbers are busy

i dream i have an audience
crowding a large theatre
the red velvet is swept aside
and i appear in a satin gown
looking like Margaret Atwood
with everyone asking me to recite
at dinner

the unsaid

the brilliant language of motion
stirs my morning coffee
sugars silenced conversation
between the sipping and
the inside of clarity

incomprehensible slopes
cover decorum
with dark imagination
compresses thirsty words
in a total eclipse
leaving gaping perditions
where the unspoken
dreams gather

remote promises remain
unfulfilled
starved in their own memories
the size of a china mug

the constant
pervasion
brews a poem
spilling over yesterday
leaving perfect stains
unsaid

I Sew At Night

by the touch
lamp on the hexagon
where the piano
used to stand
or on the arborite
under a bright hat
in front of the patio
but only on sunny days
on the white lawn chair

I keep sewing
for charities
fight depression with needles
and brightly coloured floss
and even though the picture
of me sewing is
not what I am
sewing the reproduction
without infringing on anyone

one picture
with soft pastels
and a warm oak frame
sat among wine bottles
baseball tickets
imported perfume
and gourmet cookbooks
on the edge
without one single bid

for numberless hours
I strained my eyes
and my back
waiting to see if anyone would

finally someone did

When He Died, He Took One Last Poem With Him

For Earle Birney

He lived his life like a leaf
dancing and singing
from a hazel bough
In winter, he'd simply move
the tree indoors

His words etched
a million faces on paper
burned a memory
in metaphor
cities of parchment
exploded like fire crackers

His hands moulded pictures
like a sculptor he'd fashion
shadows in holes
and everyone would gasp
at their exactness
The ritual was a myth

He sleeps with one last poem
as a blanket to cover
the decay of genius
now and forever

beret days
for Ted

yesterday
the sky wore
white and grey
puffy hats
a heavenly ensemble
outfit the horizon

today
the sun tilts
over one side
of my head
a bright yellow
soft velvet
round cloth
caresses my brow

tomorrow
when the darkness
fills my dreams
and the days
no longer shine
buttercups
or sings the blues
and greens
I will wear the black
with an eternal
smile

election day or Uncle Bobby

the discriminating clown
floats on parade
around City Hall
lined with spectators
constituents watching
the bulbous crimson
flags sail among billowy white
clouds of fallout

the audience lifts their faces
to circle the Head
of the beanbag raggedy man
filled with sawdust

kissing babies
passing out balloons
full of empty promises
dancing for votes
on election day

lucid eyes

the olives float
in a cocktail
you swallow
every word

in a bar
my man has left me
to relieve himself
two lucid eyes
take his chair

my man
has his own
lucid eyes
grabbing at him
as he leaves
the men's room

"how about a drink?"

i emptied my glass
of flattery

my depression

my depression is a page in your book

the words flow into the night
of rivers and dark passages
written long ago

I turn the page and find you
between the lines
you cradle me
as one cradles pain

the book feels eternally safe

I move consciously
not able to find peace
until silence alters the volume
of things
my repressed guilt
reaches the colour of blood

the climax is my image
carved into a cameo
around my throat
choked up

Israel

neon tourists
religiously crowd
important land
jealously guarded
by five Arabian nations

metal green soldiers
with tender faces of spring
quietly march uneasy streets
carrying experienced guns

the security mighty
as the ancient stone
forever supporting
the left, the centre and the right
wings radically worn
as an orthodoxy
under constant prayers
for peace

Sewing Jesus

I am sewing Jesus with TLC

I am bringing Jesus back to life
filling holes with tangible substance
creating a miracle
masterpiece from canvas and thread

In Jerusalem, Jesus graces
the church wall
tiny painted porcelain squares
thousands
of people from all over the world
line up for hours
burn incense   light candles
kneel down and pray
to the mosaic messiah

No one will kneel down and pray to my Jesus
cross-stitched   stretched and hung
on Franca's living room wall
next to Rosary beads and a bible

if I was sewing Jesus in the church
maybe
the Pope would deify Him
take Him to the Vatican
place Him on the church wall
next to Rosary beads and a bible
burn incense   light candles
and thousands of people
from all over the world
would line up for hours
kneel down and pray
to the framed cross
stitched saviour

The Budgie

i imagine i lived once before
not as a human being,
but as a delicate blue budgie
content with a sheltered existence
in a metal cage.

this explains why i am never eager
to make flight to far away places
or yearn for the open sky.

i must seem boring.

i love to sing
lullabies and sonnets
softened by sunlight
on a breeze in slow motion.

i spend hours
minding my own business
not to ruffle any feathers
or hurt anyone's feelings.

i must have been that sensitive budgie
whose music concealed the fear
of darkness
and sudden anger

and displayed the genteel
dignity of an orchid.

The Dead Sea

swept across the edge
yellow rocks and sand
hug blue and grey snakes
rippling gently

in the silver mist
the silent landscape
elegantly drapes
the phantom camouflage
of an ancient haze

Bedouins camp in meagre huts
rich in culture
beside busy highways
dividing
the present and the past

resting on authoritative mountains
deserted stone fortresses keep
watch over the eternal history
buried in biblical caves
by valiant ancestors

the mist and the sea kiss
in the sunlight
the sacred union
transforms the centuries
into a panorama of mystery

the melancholy moon

meanders
in and out
of cloud shadows
pale grey
radiating
half
the smile

lazily coasting
the night sky
no direct path
no planned course
no charted destination
from my aimless journey

no wonder i am tired
of appearing happy

upwards on windy stairs

i am like the mist
creeping softly
behind the hills
among cloud shadows
winding my way
home

the scorpion hustles
like the moon tides
slurring patterns
up and down
continuously
when the mood is right

i am changing
places quietly
on the cusp
between horizons
and seconds come
and go without a place
to go

pushing upwards
like dust and debris
the scorpion is worn down
little by little
struggling in shadows
on windy stairs

Why Did They Hang The Poet?

for Ken Saro-Wiwa & Nobel Prize Winner Wole Soyinka

the long standing friction
between elections and literature
has been arrested
and crushed
under a rock

there was no hesitation
in the decision
a strong and mighty army
carefully crafted
a composition of iron fists
in Nigeria

the world cried the day
the poetry suffered
a cruel and senseless execution
the Nobel Prize was found
guilty of treason
and left to rot in a vacuum
of corruption

guerrillas on horseback
fixed the noose
securely around the award
strangled an entire nation

fortunately, there will always be
another ambitious poet writing
in the wings

With No Sympathy

morning bursts open
like a chestnut in the microwave
smears ultra-yellow all over
my face
with fiery passion
bringing no warmth

the sun hunts me down
like a trained dog
burrows into my pillow
sniffs me out
from under my covers
drags my shivering body
from my bed
to the mercy of the ceramic
and the porcelain

anxiety attack

a sickening slumber
groans hollow
in the pit
of my stomach

nightmares gallop
across the terrain
thundering
hoofs dig constantly
in the dark
alleyways
my mind
always vigilant
ticking like a clock

the animal
licks its wounds
in the corner
of my heart

down in teawee land

the cyber addict
sifts through fast
different times
on the west coast

San Francisco is big
on waves
of habits
since the 1960's

the first computer
-ized flower power
then the Word
love grew like a malignancy
developed major plots
brainwashed the public
into buying
an Apple a day

Between Montreal and Toronto

the land of the bilingual
signs advertise haute stuff

along the Q.E.W.
the roads are free
(no fences to sit on)
enough
lanes for three Mack trucks
side by side by side speed
in unity do *vantastic* wheelies
roll off   knock down a few cars
steer-ike on the giant bowling alley

even the cows
understand two belles-lettres
in idealistic meadows
that have seen too many collisions

some never read the signs
eyes closed to the miles
of dust raised at cabinet meetings
where language is *haute* stuff

throngs of assimilated people
cram the legislature
where the bilingualism all began

the market

last week's fresh meat
is lined up in bulk

the price freeze
controls the quality
weighed behind
the political window

"hey you, take a number
wait your turn to be served"

the cost of poverty escalates
striking
signs scream neon
bargains widespread
on every street corner live
stock slashed

no one is in the line
for good

The Trucker on The 401

roadie in red shirt, black hat, yellow
teeth and fingers
rides the lane
noisy rollicking steamroller
will not be swayed

sashays down the highway
flicking sardonic ashes
under exalted wheels
with *savoir faire*

pulls away
my thoughts   trail
smoke and exhaust
rise in chorus
sings to the cumbrous sawhorse
cutting up the road

in the common calamity of road rage,
hurled rocks, guns and hunting knives,
the trucker on the 401
rolled up
shirtsleeves and windows
continues to drive
with reckless abandon

turning grey in summer

i know what men want
obsessed with beauty
thin enough to pass
through a needle

i dress each day
pretending to be size 8
squeeze into clothes
ten years too tight

someone else stares at me
through the glass
a pathetic woman turns
grey like the sky
in mist and fog

i imagine blue and yellow
catch sunlight
drown
in the grey
of a cloud

earlier in summer
men watched me shine
the colour of a snapdragon
after the rain